GRABOVOI CODES FOR MIND, STRESS & EMOTIONAL BALANCE

BOOK 2

Disclaimer & Safety Notice

This book addresses mental, emotional, and nervous-system balance using numerical focus techniques commonly referred to as Grabovoi Codes.

These practices are **not a substitute** for medical treatment, therapy, or crisis intervention.

If you are experiencing severe depression, suicidal thoughts, psychosis, or dissociation, **do not rely solely on this material**. Seek immediate professional or emergency support.

Do **not** use these techniques while driving, operating machinery, or during moments requiring full external attention.

Grounding practices are included throughout this book and should not be skipped.

Dedication

For those who carry invisible weight.
For the ones who keep functioning while silently overwhelmed.
And for anyone learning how to steady the mind without losing themselves.

"The nervous system remembers what the mind tries to forget."
— Anonymous

The Grabovoi Codes — Practical Applications Series is designed as a progressive trilogy:

- **Book I:** *Health & Body Repair*
- **Book II:** *Mind, Stress & Emotional Balance*
- **Book III:** *Reality Alignment & Life Systems*

Each volume builds independently but works best as part of the complete system.

How to Use This Book

This is not a book to rush.

Each chapter introduces:

- A specific mental or emotional state
- Corresponding numerical sequences
- Practical methods for daily use
- Safety and grounding guidance

You may read cover-to-cover or jump directly to the sections that apply to your current state.

Consistency matters more than intensity.

Short, calm focus is more effective than forced repetition.

Table of Contents

Chapter 1 — The Nervous System Under Pressure
Chapter 2 — Stress, Overload, and Mental Fatigue
Chapter 3 — Anxiety Patterns and Hypervigilance
Chapter 4 — Emotional Suppression and Internal Conflict
Chapter 5 — Sleep Disruption and Mental Exhaustion

Chapter 6 — Panic States and Acute Stress Response
Chapter 7 — Emotional Memory and Residual Trauma
Chapter 8 — Focus Loss, Brain Fog, and Cognitive Drift
Chapter 9 — Irritability, Emotional Volatility, and Burnout
Chapter 10 — Fear Loops and Anticipatory Anxiety

Chapter 11 — Depression, Low Motivation, and Emotional
Numbness
Chapter 12 — Addiction Triggers and Relapse Warning States
Chapter 13 — Grief, Loss, and Emotional Shock
Chapter 14 — Intrusive Thoughts and Mental Noise
Chapter 15 — Emotional Detachment and Dissociation

Chapter 16 — Nervous System Reset Protocols
Chapter 17 — Emotional Stability During Crisis
Chapter 18 — Daily Emotional Regulation Practices
Chapter 19 — Long-Term Mental Balance Strategies
Chapter 20 — Integration, Grounding, and Safe Continuation

Appendix A — Relapse Warning Signals
Appendix B — Grounding Techniques & Safety Checklist
Appendix C — Daily Use Schedules
Final Notes from the Author

Chapter 1

The Nervous System Under Pressure**

The modern nervous system is rarely at rest.

Even in moments that appear calm on the surface, the body is often operating in a low-level state of alert. Muscles remain slightly tense. Breathing stays shallow. Thoughts continue to scan for problems, obligations, or threats that may not even exist yet.

This is not a personal failure.
It is a conditioned response.

The nervous system evolved to react to danger, not to constant stimulation. When it is exposed to ongoing stress—work pressure, financial uncertainty, emotional strain, digital overload—it adapts by staying partially activated at all times. Over weeks and months, this becomes the new baseline.

The result is a system that no longer knows how to fully power down.

How Pressure Builds in the Nervous System

Stress is not only emotional. It is physiological.

When pressure accumulates, the nervous system begins to show predictable patterns:

- Heightened sensitivity to noise, light, or interruption
- Difficulty relaxing even during rest
- Racing thoughts without a clear cause

- Sudden fatigue followed by bursts of anxious energy
- A feeling of being "on edge" without knowing why

These symptoms often appear long before a person consciously identifies themselves as stressed.

At this stage, the body is not asking for motivation or willpower. It is asking for regulation.

Why Mental Control Often Makes Things Worse

Many people respond to nervous-system overload by trying to think their way out of it.

They force positivity.
They suppress anxiety.
They push through exhaustion.

This creates a secondary problem.

When the mind attempts to override the nervous system instead of stabilizing it, internal conflict increases. The body senses danger while the mind insists there is none. This mismatch amplifies stress signals rather than reducing them.

True regulation works from the inside out, not the other way around.

Numerical Focus as a Stabilizing Tool

Grabovoi Codes, when applied correctly, are not about forcing change.

They act as **anchors**—points of neutral focus that interrupt runaway stress loops.

The nervous system responds to rhythm, repetition, and consistency. Numerical focus provides all three without emotional charge. Unlike affirmations, numbers do not provoke resistance or disbelief. They are processed quietly, without argument.

When used gently, they help the nervous system exit constant alert mode and return toward balance.

Core Code for Nervous System Stabilization

Primary Code:
548 721

This sequence is used to support general nervous-system regulation during periods of sustained pressure.

How to Use

- Sit or lie down comfortably
- Breathe slowly through the nose
- Gently focus on the sequence **548 721**
- Do not rush or force clarity
- Allow the numbers to repeat naturally

Practice for **3–5 minutes**, once or twice daily.

If thoughts wander, simply return to the sequence without judgment.

Sensations You May Notice

During or after use, it is common to experience:

- A subtle slowing of thought
- A drop in physical tension
- Deeper or more regular breathing
- Mild emotional release (sighing, yawning, heaviness)

These are signs the nervous system is shifting out of high alert.

If discomfort arises, stop the session and ground yourself by focusing on physical surroundings.

Important Safety Note

Do not attempt long sessions when first starting.

Short, consistent exposure is more effective than extended focus. Overuse can cause temporary fatigue or emotional sensitivity in some individuals.

Stability comes from repetition, not intensity.

Chapter 2

Stress Overload and Mental Fatigue**

Mental fatigue is not the same as tiredness.

A person can sleep for eight hours and still wake up mentally exhausted. Thoughts feel heavy. Focus is scattered. Simple decisions require effort. Motivation drops, not because of laziness, but because the mind is overloaded.

This state develops gradually. Most people do not notice it until their ability to cope suddenly collapses.

What Mental Fatigue Really Is

Mental fatigue occurs when the nervous system has been processing stress signals for too long without resolution.

This includes:

- Ongoing worry
- Emotional suppression
- Information overload
- Repetitive problem-solving with no clear outcome
- Constant background anxiety

The brain was never designed to run continuously at this level. When it does, efficiency drops. Memory weakens. Emotional regulation becomes unstable.

Importantly, this is not psychological weakness.
It is neurological saturation.

The Loop Effect

One of the most damaging aspects of stress overload is the **loop effect**.

The same thoughts repeat.
The same concerns resurface.
The same internal conversations replay.

The mind attempts to solve problems that may not have immediate solutions. Each loop consumes energy, even when no progress is made. Over time, this creates a sense of mental "pressure," as if the brain cannot fully clear itself.

This is often when people describe feeling:

- Foggy
- Detached
- Irritable
- Emotionally flat
- Unable to concentrate

At this stage, rest alone is not enough. The looping must be interrupted.

Why Rest Sometimes Fails

Many people are confused when relaxation techniques do not work.

They sit down.
They breathe.
They try to calm their thoughts.

But the mind continues racing.

This happens because mental fatigue is not caused by lack of rest—it is caused by **unresolved activation**. The system is still running internal processes in the background.

The solution is not suppression.
It is redirection.

Numerical Interruption of Cognitive Overload

Grabovoi Codes can be used as a neutral interrupt signal.

Numbers do not demand belief.
They do not trigger emotional resistance.
They give the mind something precise to hold onto.

When focused on gently, numerical sequences reduce the brain's tendency to replay stress loops by occupying cognitive bandwidth in a non-threatening way.

Core Code for Mental Fatigue and Overthinking

Primary Code:
719 834

This sequence is used to reduce repetitive thought patterns and mental exhaustion.

How to Use

- Sit upright or recline comfortably

- Keep breathing slow and natural
- Focus lightly on **719 834**
- Allow the numbers to repeat internally
- Do not visualize outcomes or force calm

Use for **3–7 minutes**, once daily.

This code works best after periods of intense mental activity or before sleep.

Signs the Code Is Working

You may notice:

- Thoughts slowing without effort
- A feeling of mental "space" opening
- Reduced urgency to solve problems
- Gentle tiredness rather than agitation

These responses indicate the mind is stepping out of overload mode.

Avoiding Common Mistakes

Do not:

- Stack multiple codes at once
- Force concentration
- Use the sequence while emotionally overwhelmed

If emotions rise sharply, pause the session and ground yourself first.

Stability always comes before expansion.

Chapter 3

Emotional Strain Stored in the Body**

Emotional stress does not stay in the mind.

When emotions are suppressed, delayed, or ignored, they are carried by the body instead. Muscles tighten. Breathing changes. Hormonal responses remain active longer than necessary. Over time, this creates physical patterns that persist even when the original emotional trigger is gone.

This is why people often feel tense, tired, or unwell without being able to identify a clear emotional cause.

The body remembers what the mind has moved past.

How Emotional Load Becomes Physical

Emotions activate the nervous system. When they are fully expressed and resolved, the system returns to baseline.

When they are not, the activation remains.

Common examples include:

- Holding anger to avoid conflict
- Suppressing fear to appear capable
- Ignoring grief to continue functioning
- Dismissing sadness as weakness

Each time this happens, the body absorbs the unfinished response.

Over time, this can manifest as:

- Chronic tension in the neck, jaw, or shoulders
- Digestive disruption
- Shallow breathing
- Persistent fatigue
- Heightened sensitivity to stress

These symptoms are not imaginary. They are the physical residue of unresolved emotional signaling.

Why Talking Alone Is Sometimes Not Enough

Talking about emotions can help clarify experiences, but it does not always discharge stored activation.

This is because emotional strain is often **pre-verbal**. It lives in bodily responses that formed before conscious reasoning had a chance to intervene.

For this reason, approaches that work directly with attention and regulation can be especially effective.

Numerical focus operates at this level.

Using Numerical Focus to Release Stored Emotional Load

Grabovoi Codes do not force emotional release.

They create a neutral focus point that allows the nervous system to relax its grip gradually. When attention stabilizes without pressure, the body is more willing to let go of stored tension.

This process is subtle. It does not require reliving events or intensifying emotions.

Release happens quietly.

Core Code for Emotional Strain and Internal Pressure

Primary Code:
814 542

This sequence is used to support emotional unloading and body-based stress release.

How to Use

- Sit or lie down comfortably
- Place one hand on your chest or abdomen
- Focus gently on **814 542**
- Allow breathing to slow naturally
- Do not try to "feel" anything specific

Practice for **5 minutes**, once daily.

If emotional responses arise, allow them without analysis.

Common Responses During Use

You may experience:

- Deep sighs or yawning
- Sudden warmth or heaviness
- Mild emotional release without clear thoughts

- Temporary fatigue followed by clarity

These responses indicate the nervous system is discharging stored tension.

If sensations become intense, shorten the session and return to grounding practices.

Important Boundaries

Do not use this code during acute emotional crisis.

Stabilize first. Regulation must precede release.

This work is about restoring balance—not opening floodgates.

Emotional strain does not mean you are fragile.

It means your system has been carrying more than it should alone.

Chapter 4

Sleep Disruption and Nighttime Nervous System Activity**

Sleep problems are rarely just about sleep.

They are often the result of a nervous system that does not know when it is safe to power down.

Many people report exhaustion but cannot fall asleep. Others fall asleep easily but wake repeatedly. Some wake at the same hour every night with a racing mind or physical tension.

These patterns are not random.

They reflect unresolved activation in the body's regulation systems.

Why the Body Resists Sleep

Sleep requires a shift from alertness to repair.

When the nervous system remains in a low-level threat state, it keeps scanning, even during rest. This can be triggered by:

- Chronic stress
- Emotional suppression
- Physical pain
- Irregular routines
- Long-term anxiety patterns

The mind may feel calm, but the body has not received the signal to stand down.

This is why traditional sleep advice often fails. The problem is not discipline. It is regulation.

The Role of Nighttime Awareness

At night, external distractions drop away.

What remains is internal signaling.

If the body has been storing stress, nighttime becomes the moment it finally tries to process it. This can appear as:

- Sudden thoughts or memories
- Physical restlessness
- Chest tightness
- Shallow breathing
- Temperature changes

These are not signs of danger. They are signs of delayed processing.

Numerical Focus as a Sleep Regulator

Grabovoi Codes can be used to signal safety to the nervous system without effort.

Unlike affirmations or visualization, numerical focus does not require emotional engagement. It gives the system something stable to rest on.

This allows sleep to arrive naturally.

Core Code for Sleep Regulation

Primary Code:
918 794

This sequence is used to support nervous system downshifting and sleep initiation.

How to Use

- Use while lying in bed
- Do not force concentration
- Gently repeat or visualize **918 794**
- Allow attention to drift

If sleep does not come immediately, continue calmly for **5–10 minutes**.

Stop once drowsiness increases.

Waking During the Night

If you wake suddenly or at the same time each night, do not check the clock.

Clock-watching reinforces alertness.

Instead:

- Place attention on slow breathing
- Return focus to **918 794**
- Let the body re-enter rest

Most people fall back asleep without realizing it.

Common Effects Over Time

With consistent use, people often report:

- Falling asleep faster
- Fewer nighttime awakenings
- Deeper, more restorative sleep
- Reduced morning tension

These changes tend to appear gradually over several nights.

Important Guidance

Do not combine this practice with stimulants, heavy screen use, or emotionally charged material before bed.

Sleep regulation works best when the body is not being pulled in opposing directions.

Sleep is not something to force.

It is something the body allows when it feels safe enough to let go.

Chapter 5

Chronic Fatigue and Energy Depletion**

Chronic fatigue is not simply tiredness.

It is a state where the body no longer recovers properly, even after rest.

People experiencing it often hear advice to "push through" or "get more sleep," yet neither solves the problem. In many cases, effort makes symptoms worse.

This is because chronic fatigue is usually a **regulation issue**, not a motivation issue.

Understanding Energy Depletion

The body produces energy continuously, but it also consumes energy to maintain balance.

When stress, illness, emotional strain, or prolonged overexertion is present, the body diverts energy toward survival functions rather than repair.

Over time, this creates patterns such as:

- Feeling exhausted after minor tasks
- Brain fog or slow thinking
- Heavy limbs
- Sensitivity to noise or light
- Energy "crashes" after activity

The system is not broken. It is conserving.

Why Rest Alone Isn't Enough

Rest helps, but rest does not automatically reset regulatory patterns.

If the nervous system remains in a guarded state, recovery processes stay partially offline. This is why some people can rest all day and still feel depleted.

The missing signal is **permission to restore**.

Numerical Focus for Energy Stabilization

Grabovoi Codes can be used to gently support energy balance without forcing output.

The goal is not stimulation. It is **efficiency**.

When the body uses energy more efficiently, fatigue decreases naturally.

Core Code for Energy Restoration

Primary Code:
481 241

This sequence is used to support balanced energy production and reduce exhaustion patterns.

How to Use

- Sit or lie comfortably

- Focus lightly on **481 241**
- Do not "push" attention
- Use for **5 minutes**, once or twice daily

Morning or early afternoon is ideal.

Managing Activity Without Crashing

When recovering from fatigue, pacing matters more than intensity.

Use this simple guideline:

- Stop activity **before** exhaustion
- Allow short recovery periods
- Resume gently

Using the code **481 241** after activity can help reduce post-exertion crashes.

Emotional Fatigue and Energy Loss

Unexpressed or prolonged emotional strain consumes significant energy.

This often appears as:

- Feeling "drained" by conversations
- Avoidance of social contact
- Irritability without clear cause

Numerical focus can be helpful here because it does not require emotional processing.

The body can release tension without revisiting the source.

What to Expect Over Time

With consistent use, many people report:

- Fewer energy crashes
- More stable daily stamina
- Improved mental clarity
- Less need for stimulants

These changes are typically gradual and cumulative.

Important Note

Do not increase activity suddenly because you feel better.

Energy recovery works best when gains are respected, not tested.

The body responds to safety and consistency.

Chapter 6

Digestive Stress and Gut Regulation**

Digestive issues are rarely isolated to the gut.

They are often signals of how the nervous system is responding to stress, safety, and control.

Many people treat digestion as a mechanical problem — something to fix with restriction, elimination, or constant monitoring. While diet matters, digestion is also deeply **regulatory**.

The gut listens to the brain.

How Stress Affects Digestion

The digestive system is one of the first areas affected when the body feels unsafe.

When stress is present, the body prioritizes survival over digestion. Blood flow shifts away from the gut, enzymes reduce, and motility changes.

Common signs include:

- Bloating without clear cause
- Irregular bowel movements
- Nausea or heaviness after eating
- Food sensitivities that fluctuate
- Appetite changes

These symptoms often worsen during emotional strain — even when diet stays the same.

The Gut–Nervous System Link

The gut contains a dense network of nerves often referred to as the "second brain."

When the nervous system is overstimulated or fatigued, digestive signals become inconsistent. This can lead to cycles of:

- Over-monitoring food
- Anxiety around meals
- Restriction followed by flare-ups

The system becomes reactive instead of responsive.

Regulation Over Restriction

Excessive control can increase digestive stress.

Constantly analyzing food, symptoms, and timing sends a signal of threat rather than support. The body responds by tightening further.

The goal is **regulation**, not perfection.

Numerical focus offers a way to support digestion without forcing change.

Core Code for Digestive Balance

Primary Code:
918 794

This sequence is used to support calm digestive signaling and improved gut coordination.

How to Use

- Use before or after meals
- Sit comfortably and breathe normally
- Focus lightly on **918 794**
- Duration: **3–5 minutes**

No visualization is required.

Reducing Meal-Related Tension

If meals cause anxiety or discomfort:

- Use the code **before eating**, not during symptoms
- Keep attention relaxed
- Avoid multitasking during focus

This helps the body shift into a receptive state.

Digestive Symptoms That Fluctuate

Symptoms that change day-to-day are often regulatory rather than structural.

If tests show no clear pathology, this does not mean the symptoms are imagined. It means the system is dynamic.

Supporting regulation can reduce intensity even when the root cause is unclear.

Supporting Digestion Without Overdoing It

Helpful practices:

- Eat at consistent times
- Avoid rushing meals
- Sit upright after eating
- Limit symptom-tracking obsession

Numerical focus works best alongside **simplicity**.

What Improvement Often Looks Like

Progress may appear as:

- Less bloating overall
- Faster symptom recovery
- Fewer food reactions
- Reduced anxiety around eating

Digestive healing is rarely linear. Small improvements still matter.

Important Note

If digestive pain is severe, persistent, or worsening, medical evaluation is essential.

Numerical focus is **supportive**, not a replacement for diagnosis or care.

In the next chapter, we will explore **sleep disruption and nervous system overactivity**, and how to encourage restorative rest without pressure.

Chapter 7

Sleep Disruption and Nervous System Overactivity**

Sleep problems are rarely just about sleep.

They are usually signals that the nervous system is overstimulated, under-recovered, or stuck in a heightened state of alert.

Many people approach sleep issues by forcing routines, tracking metrics obsessively, or becoming anxious about "getting enough." This often makes the problem worse.

Sleep cannot be commanded.
It has to be **allowed**.

Why the Body Resists Sleep

Sleep requires a sense of safety.

When the nervous system perceives threat — physical, emotional, or psychological — the body stays partially awake, even when exhausted.

Common signs of nervous system–driven sleep disruption include:

- Difficulty falling asleep despite fatigue
- Waking at the same time every night
- Light, fragmented sleep
- Vivid or stressful dreams
- Feeling "tired but wired"

These patterns are regulatory, not moral failures or lack of discipline.

Hypervigilance and Nighttime Awareness

For many people, nighttime is when unprocessed stress surfaces.

The absence of distraction allows the nervous system to scan internally. Thoughts speed up. Sensations become louder. Small discomforts feel amplified.

Trying to "force calm" often increases alertness.

The goal is **downshifting**, not shutdown.

Why Effort Backfires at Night

Sleep improves when effort decreases.

Actively trying to fall asleep tells the brain something is wrong. This keeps the system engaged.

Numerical focus works best when it is:

- Passive
- Short
- Non-goal-oriented

You are not trying to sleep.
You are giving the system a neutral point to rest on.

Core Code for Sleep Regulation

Primary Code:
715 821

This sequence is used to support nervous system settling and reduce internal alertness before sleep.

How to Use

- Use while lying down or seated
- Focus gently on **715 821**
- Let attention drift naturally
- Duration: **3–7 minutes**

If you fall asleep during use, stop. There is no need to "finish."

When to Use the Code

Effective times include:

- 30–60 minutes before bed
- After waking during the night
- During periods of mental overstimulation

Avoid using it while actively anxious about sleep. If tension is high, wait until it eases slightly.

Night Waking and Re-Entry

Waking during the night is not failure.

It is often the nervous system checking its environment.

If you wake:

- Do not check the time
- Avoid phone screens

- Use light focus on the code
- Keep breathing natural

The goal is **returning to neutrality**, not forcing rest.

What Sleep Improvement Often Looks Like

Progress may show up as:

- Falling asleep without noticing when it happens
- Shorter night awakenings
- Less urgency around bedtime
- Feeling slightly more rested, even with the same hours

These subtle shifts signal regulation returning.

Reducing Sleep Obsession

Tracking every detail of sleep can increase pressure.

If you notice fixation increasing:

- Take breaks from sleep apps
- Focus on daytime regulation
- Use numerical focus earlier in the evening

Sleep improves when it stops being the central project.

Important Note

Persistent insomnia, sleep apnea symptoms, or sudden changes in sleep patterns require medical attention.

Numerical focus supports regulation — it does not diagnose or treat sleep disorders.

In the next chapter, we will address **chronic fatigue and low energy states**, and how to support recovery without pushing the body beyond its limits.

Chapter 8

Chronic Fatigue and Energy Depletion**

Chronic fatigue is not the same as being tired.

Tiredness improves with rest.
Chronic fatigue persists **despite** rest.

For many people, it feels like the body never fully recharges — as if energy is leaking faster than it can be restored.

This state is not weakness.
It is often a sign of prolonged nervous system strain.

Understanding Energy Beyond Sleep

Energy is regulated across multiple systems:

- Nervous system tone
- Hormonal balance
- Immune signaling
- Emotional load

When these systems remain under stress for long periods, the body shifts into a conservation mode.

This can look like:

- Heavy limbs
- Brain fog
- Low motivation
- Sensitivity to noise or light
- Crashes after small efforts

The body is not failing.
It is protecting itself.

Why Pushing Makes Fatigue Worse

Many people respond to fatigue by pushing harder.

They force productivity.
They override signals.
They "power through."

Short-term, this can work.
Long-term, it deepens depletion.

Each override teaches the nervous system that rest is unsafe or unavailable.

Recovery begins when the body feels **permission** to restore.

The Role of Nervous System Drain

Chronic stress keeps the nervous system partially activated.

Even when sitting still, the body may be spending energy maintaining alertness.

Signs of this include:

- Feeling exhausted but restless
- Difficulty relaxing without distraction
- Needing stimulation just to function

This constant background activation drains reserves quietly.

Core Code for Energy Stabilization

Primary Code:
498 713

This sequence is used to support energy stabilization and reduce internal drain.

It is not a stimulant.
It works by easing unnecessary energy expenditure.

How to Use

- Sit or lie down comfortably
- Focus gently on **498 713**
- Keep attention light
- Duration: **3–6 minutes**

Stop if you feel pressure to "make it work."

Best Times to Use

This code is most effective:

- Midday, before fatigue peaks
- After mental or emotional exertion
- During recovery days

Avoid using it late at night if you are sensitive to mental clarity increases.

What Recovery Often Feels Like

Improvement may appear subtly:

- Less heaviness in the body
- Slightly clearer thinking
- Reduced need to "push"
- More stable energy across the day

These changes often precede noticeable increases in stamina.

Redefining Productivity During Recovery

Recovery phases require a different metric of success.

Instead of asking:
"How much did I do?"

Ask:
"How much did I *not* force?"

Respecting limits restores energy faster than ignoring them.

When to Seek Medical Support

Chronic fatigue that is:

- Sudden
- Severe
- Accompanied by pain, weight loss, or fever

should always be evaluated medically.

Numerical focus supports regulation — it does not replace medical care.

Closing Thought

Energy returns when the body feels safe enough to release control.

In the next chapter, we will explore **digestive stress and gut– nervous system connection**, and how internal tension often shows up in digestion before anywhere else.

Chapter 9

Digestive Stress and the Gut–Nervous System Link**

Digestive problems are rarely just digestive.

The gut is one of the most sensitive mirrors of nervous system stress. When tension becomes chronic, digestion is often the first system to react.

This can include:

- Bloating
- Tightness or cramping
- Nausea
- Irregular appetite
- Sudden food sensitivities

These symptoms are signals — not failures.

Why Stress Hits the Gut First

The digestive system is governed by the **enteric nervous system**, sometimes called the "second brain."

It communicates constantly with:

- The vagus nerve
- Stress hormones
- Immune signaling

When the body senses threat — physical or emotional — digestion becomes a lower priority.

Blood flow shifts away from the gut.
Motility changes.
Enzymes decrease.

The body prepares for survival, not digestion.

The Cost of Long-Term Digestive Tension

Short-term digestive stress resolves quickly.

Long-term tension does not.

Over time, this may feel like:

- Food sitting "too long"
- Sudden intolerance to meals that were once fine
- A constant sense of heaviness after eating
- Alternating constipation and urgency

These patterns often reflect **nervous system dysregulation**, not structural damage.

The Gut as an Emotional Sensor

The gut reacts strongly to unresolved emotion.

Anxiety often shows up as:

- Tightness
- Nausea
- Loss of appetite

Suppressed emotion can appear as:

- Sluggish digestion
- Bloating
- Comfort eating followed by discomfort

The body stores what the mind avoids.

Core Code for Digestive Regulation

Primary Code:
812 619

This sequence is used to support digestive calm and nervous system coordination.

Its role is to reduce internal tension that interferes with normal gut rhythms.

How to Use

- Sit upright or lie on your left side
- Place attention on the abdomen
- Gently focus on **812 619**
- Duration: **3–5 minutes**

No visualization is required.

When to Use This Code

This code works best:

- Before meals
- After emotional stress
- During digestive discomfort not linked to illness

Avoid using immediately after very heavy meals.

What Improvement Often Looks Like

Digestive recovery is gradual.

Common early signs include:

- Reduced tightness
- Easier bowel movements
- Less urgency
- More predictable appetite

The goal is stability, not perfection.

Supporting Digestion Without Forcing

Helpful habits include:

- Eating without screens
- Slower chewing
- Smaller portions during recovery
- Pausing between meals

Forcing "clean eating" during stress often worsens symptoms.

Medical Considerations

Persistent digestive symptoms should always be assessed medically, especially if accompanied by:

- Blood
- Severe pain
- Sudden weight loss

Numerical focus supports regulation — it does not diagnose or treat disease.

Closing Thought

Digestion improves when the body no longer feels rushed or threatened.

In the next chapter, we will explore **sleep disruption and nighttime nervous system activity**, and why rest can feel elusive even when exhaustion is present.

Chapter 10

Sleep Disruption and Night-Time Nervous System Activity**

Sleep problems are rarely about sleep alone.

They are usually the nervous system refusing to fully stand down.

People experiencing nervous system overload often report:

- Trouble falling asleep
- Waking between 2–4 a.m.
- Shallow or fragmented sleep
- Feeling tired but wired

The body rests, but the system stays alert.

Why the Body Won't "Switch Off"

Sleep requires a shift from **sympathetic activation** (alert mode) to **parasympathetic dominance** (rest mode).

When this transition fails, the body remains partially guarded.

Common causes include:

- Prolonged stress
- Emotional suppression
- Irregular sleep routines
- Excess stimulation late in the evening

The nervous system interprets night-time stillness as unsafe rather than restorative.

The 2–4 a.m. Wake Pattern

Many people wake repeatedly during this window.

This is not random.

During these hours:

- Cortisol begins to rise
- The liver and nervous system exchange regulatory signals
- Emotional processing becomes more active

If unresolved tension exists, the body wakes to monitor it.

Why Exhaustion Doesn't Guarantee Sleep

Sleep is not caused by fatigue alone.

It requires:

- Safety
- Predictability
- Nervous system permission

When vigilance is high, exhaustion can actually worsen sleep quality.

The body stays half-awake "just in case."

Core Code for Sleep Regulation

Primary Code:
739 218

This sequence is used to support night-time nervous system settling and smoother sleep transitions.

It is not a sedative.
It works by reducing internal alert signaling.

How to Use

- Use only in the evening
- Sit or lie comfortably
- Focus gently on **739 218**
- Duration: **5 minutes**

Avoid repeating excessively.

When to Use This Code

Best times:

- 30–60 minutes before bed
- After emotional stimulation
- After long periods of mental overactivity

Do not use while driving or during tasks requiring alertness.

Creating a Sleep-Friendly Environment

Small changes matter more than drastic ones.

Helpful supports:

- Dim lights after sunset
- No phone use in bed
- Consistent bedtime
- Cool room temperature

Sleep routines teach the nervous system what to expect.

What Improvement Usually Looks Like

Progress is often subtle:

- Falling asleep faster
- Fewer night awakenings
- Easier return to sleep
- More rested feeling upon waking

Sleep stabilizes before it deepens.

Medical Considerations

Persistent insomnia, sleep apnea symptoms, or severe sleep disturbance should be medically assessed.

Numerical focus supports regulation — it does not replace clinical care.

Closing Thought

The body sleeps best when it no longer feels the need to watch.

In the next chapter, we will explore **emotional release cycles** and why improvement sometimes comes with temporary emotional waves.

Chapter 11

Emotional Release Cycles and Temporary Instability**

Improvement does not always feel calm.

When the nervous system begins to regulate, stored emotional tension can surface before it settles.

This is not regression.
It is release.

Many people misinterpret this phase and stop too early.

Why Emotions Surface During Regulation

Stress is not only mental.

It is stored in:

- Muscle tone
- Breathing patterns
- Hormonal loops
- Memory networks

When regulation improves, the body finally has the capacity to process what was previously held in suspension.

This can feel unexpected or uncomfortable.

Common Emotional Release Patterns

People often report:

- Sudden sadness without clear cause
- Irritability
- Tearfulness
- Heightened sensitivity
- Vivid memories resurfacing

These waves are usually short-lived.

They pass when not resisted.

The Risk of Over-Correction

Trying to "fix" emotions during release can prolong them.

Avoid:

- Over-analyzing feelings
- Forcing positivity
- Increasing practices aggressively
- Seeking constant reassurance

Regulation requires patience, not control.

Core Code for Emotional Stabilization

Primary Code:
514 208

This sequence is used to support emotional grounding during release phases.

It helps the system integrate rather than suppress.

How to Use

- Sit or stand comfortably
- Place attention at the center of the chest
- Focus on **514 208**
- Duration: **3–4 minutes**

Do not extend beyond recommended time.

When to Use This Code

Best used:

- During emotional surges
- After stressful conversations
- When feeling unsteady without clear reason

Not necessary during calm periods.

Supporting Emotional Integration

Helpful actions include:

- Walking
- Hydration
- Writing short notes
- Gentle stretching

Avoid intense exercise during active release.

What Resolution Looks Like

Signs of successful integration include:

- Emotional neutrality returning
- Less reactivity
- Clearer thinking
- A sense of internal space

This phase often precedes noticeable improvement in physical symptoms.

Medical Considerations

If emotional distress becomes overwhelming or persistent, professional mental health support is essential.

Numerical focus supports regulation — it does not replace therapy or clinical care.

Closing Thought

Release feels unstable only because it replaces long-held tension.

In the next chapter, we will explore **fatigue, burnout, and energy misalignment**, and why rest sometimes fails to restore energy.

Chapter 12

Fatigue, Burnout, and Energy Misalignment**

Fatigue is not always caused by lack of sleep.

Many people rest properly and still wake up exhausted.

This is often a sign of **energy misalignment**, not depletion.

Understanding Burnout Beyond Tiredness

Burnout is a regulatory failure.

It occurs when:

- Stress hormones remain elevated too long
- Recovery signals fail to activate
- The nervous system stays in a "standby" state

Sleep alone cannot fix this.

Signs of Energy Misalignment

Common indicators include:

- Feeling tired but wired
- Heavy limbs without physical exertion
- Difficulty starting tasks
- Sudden crashes during the day
- Motivation without energy, or energy without focus

These symptoms often appear together.

Why Rest Sometimes Doesn't Work

Rest restores **resources**.

Burnout disrupts **distribution**.

Energy exists, but it does not flow correctly through the system.

This misrouting keeps the body from accessing what it already has.

Nervous System Contribution

The autonomic nervous system controls:

- Energy release
- Digestion
- Focus
- Recovery

When it remains biased toward stress response, energy becomes locked into defensive patterns.

Core Code for Energy Re-Alignment

Primary Code:
418 312

This sequence supports redistribution of internal energy rather than stimulation.

It is not an energizer.
It is a realignment tool.

How to Apply the Code

- Sit upright with feet on the ground
- Focus attention just below the sternum
- Hold **418 312** mentally
- Duration: **4 minutes**

Do not combine with stimulants.

Best Times to Use

Effective when:

- Morning fatigue persists despite sleep
- Midday crashes repeat daily
- Mental clarity fades without reason

Avoid using late at night.

Supporting Practices

To enhance results:

- Light exposure early in the day
- Regular meal timing
- Gentle movement instead of naps

Avoid excessive caffeine during recovery.

What Improvement Looks Like

Signs of correction include:

- More consistent daily energy
- Reduced afternoon crashes
- Improved motivation without force
- Clearer mental engagement

Changes often appear gradually over several days.

Important Reminder

Chronic fatigue can be linked to medical conditions.

Numerical focus is supportive, not diagnostic.

Always seek professional evaluation when symptoms persist.

Closing Thought

Burnout is not weakness.

It is a signal that systems need reorganization, not pressure.

In the next chapter, we will address **sleep disturbances and nighttime nervous system activity**.

Chapter 13

Sleep Disturbances and Nighttime Nervous System Activity**

Sleep problems are rarely just about sleep.

They are often the result of a nervous system that does not fully disengage.

Why the Body Stays Awake

The body enters sleep only when it feels safe.

If stress signals remain active, the brain stays alert even when tired.

This creates:

- Difficulty falling asleep
- Light or fragmented sleep
- Early waking without restfulness

Common Nighttime Patterns

Sleep disruption often appears as:

- Racing thoughts at bedtime
- Sudden waking between 2–4 a.m.
- Vivid or repetitive dreams
- Feeling alert immediately upon waking

These patterns point to **incomplete shutdown** of stress circuits.

The Role of Cortisol Timing

Cortisol should decrease at night.

When it remains elevated:

- The brain interprets threat
- Muscles stay semi-engaged
- The heart rate fails to slow

Sleep becomes shallow and inefficient.

Why Forcing Sleep Makes It Worse

Trying to "make" sleep happen activates effort.

Effort signals alertness.

The nervous system cannot relax under pressure.

Sleep must be **allowed**, not demanded.

Core Code for Nighttime Downregulation

Primary Code:
817 214

This sequence supports nervous system disengagement and circadian alignment.

It does not sedate.
It signals safety.

How to Apply the Code

- Lie down comfortably
- Place attention at the base of the skull
- Hold **817 214** mentally
- Duration: **5 minutes**

Let attention soften rather than focus sharply.

When to Use

Best applied:

- 15–30 minutes before sleep
- After nighttime waking
- During periods of mental looping

Do not use while driving or performing tasks.

Supporting Sleep Conditions

To improve effectiveness:

- Reduce overhead lighting after sunset
- Keep sleep timing consistent
- Avoid screens in the final hour

Small changes reinforce nervous system cues.

Signs of Improvement

Progress may include:

- Easier sleep onset
- Fewer awakenings
- More restorative rest
- Reduced dream intensity

Improvements may appear within several nights.

Important Reminder

Persistent insomnia can have medical causes.

Numerical focus is complementary, not a substitute for care.

Closing Thought

Sleep is not lost.

It is waiting for the right signals.

In the next chapter, we will address **anxiety loops and repetitive thought patterns**.

Chapter 14

Anxiety Loops and Repetitive Thought Patterns**

Anxiety is not just an emotion.

It is a loop.

What an Anxiety Loop Is

An anxiety loop occurs when the brain repeatedly revisits the same thought without resolution.

The thought does not change.
The outcome does not improve.
The body remains activated.

This creates:

- Mental replay
- Constant anticipation
- Difficulty concentrating
- Physical tension without release

Why the Loop Persists

The brain evolved to solve problems.

When it cannot find a solution, it keeps checking.

This checking behavior is meant to protect you.
Instead, it exhausts the nervous system.

Anxiety is often **misdirected protection**.

The Body's Role in Mental Loops

Thought loops are not purely mental.

They are reinforced by:

- Tight breathing
- Jaw clenching
- Elevated heart rate
- Shallow posture

The body feeds the mind.
The mind feeds the body.

Why Reassurance Doesn't Work

Reassurance is temporary.

The brain accepts it briefly, then returns to scanning.

This is because the underlying signal of threat has not been resolved.

The system is asking:
"Are we safe yet?"

Interrupting the Loop Mechanism

Loops cannot be argued away.

They must be **interrupted at the signal level**, not the content level.

Changing the thought is less effective than changing the state.

Core Code for Loop Interruption

Primary Code:
319 742

This sequence is used to disrupt repetitive neural firing patterns.

It signals closure rather than suppression.

How to Apply the Code

- Sit or stand comfortably
- Place one hand on the chest
- Hold **319 742** mentally
- Breathe slowly through the nose
- Duration: **3–5 minutes**

Allow thoughts to pass without engagement.

When to Use This Code

Most effective:

- During rumination
- When thoughts repeat word-for-word
- After exposure to stressors
- Before sleep if looping begins

Avoid using during high-focus tasks.

What You May Notice

Common effects include:

- Thoughts slowing naturally
- A sense of mental "space"
- Reduced urgency
- Easier redirection of attention

Relief may be subtle at first.

Reinforcing the Reset

Support the process by:

- Reducing caffeine intake
- Taking short walks
- Exhaling longer than inhaling

Small physical cues help the nervous system settle.

Important Consideration

Persistent anxiety may require professional support.

These practices are supportive, not diagnostic or curative.

Closing Thought

Anxiety is not a flaw.

It is a signal stuck in repeat.

In the next chapter, we will explore **emotional numbness and shutdown states**.

Chapter 15

Emotional Numbness and Shutdown States**

Not all stress feels loud.

Some stress goes quiet.

Understanding Emotional Numbness

Emotional numbness is not the absence of emotion.

It is the nervous system reducing input to prevent overload.

This often presents as:

- Feeling flat or disconnected
- Lack of motivation
- Difficulty feeling pleasure or sadness
- A sense of being "behind glass"

Why Shutdown Happens

When stress remains unresolved for long periods, the system adapts.

Fight and flight require energy.
Shutdown conserves it.

This is a **protective response**, not a failure.

The Freeze Response Explained

Freeze occurs when neither escape nor action feels possible.

The body lowers:

- Emotional intensity
- Physical movement
- Cognitive engagement

This can look like calm from the outside, but it is not rest.

Common Triggers for Shutdown

Shutdown states are often triggered by:

- Prolonged anxiety
- Emotional overload
- Repeated disappointment
- Feeling trapped or powerless

The trigger may be subtle or cumulative.

Why Forcing Emotion Backfires

Trying to "feel something" rarely works.

Forcing emotion activates resistance.

The system must feel **safe enough** to reopen, not pressured.

Signals of Gradual Reawakening

Healthy reactivation begins gently.

Signs include:

- Brief moments of interest
- Mild emotional flickers
- Spontaneous sighs or yawns
- Increased body awareness

These are positive indicators.

Core Code for Emotional Reconnection

Primary Code:
812 448

This sequence supports gradual emotional re-entry without overwhelm.

It is not a stimulant.
It is a stabilizer.

How to Apply the Code

- Sit comfortably with feet on the ground
- Place one hand on the abdomen
- Hold **812 448** mentally
- Breathe slowly and evenly
- Duration: **5–7 minutes**

Do not search for emotion.
Allow whatever arises.

When to Use This Code

Best used:

- During emotional flatness
- After burnout
- During recovery periods
- When motivation feels absent

Not recommended during acute panic.

Supporting the Process

Helpful additions include:

- Gentle movement (walking, stretching)
- Warm showers or baths
- Consistent sleep routines
- Exposure to natural light

Consistency matters more than intensity.

Important Note

Emotional numbness can also be associated with depression or trauma.

Professional support is encouraged when symptoms persist.

Closing Thought

Numbness is not emptiness.

It is a pause.

In the next chapter, we will explore **regulation after emotional overload** and how stability returns in stages.

Chapter 16

Regulation After Emotional Overload**

Recovery does not happen all at once.

It happens in layers.

What Emotional Overload Really Is

Emotional overload occurs when the nervous system receives more input than it can process.

This can come from:

- Prolonged stress
- Intense emotional events
- Repeated interpersonal strain
- Unresolved internal conflict

The system does not "break."
It **downshifts**.

Why Overload Feels Different for Everyone

Some people become anxious.
Others shut down.
Some feel irritable or detached.

These are not personality traits.
They are **regulation strategies**.

Your nervous system chooses the option that costs the least energy.

The False Expectation of Immediate Relief

Many people expect recovery to feel like relief.

It usually does not.

Early regulation feels:

- Neutral
- Uneventful
- Slightly dull

This is normal.

Calm often feels boring before it feels safe.

The Three Stages of Post-Overload Regulation

1. Stabilization

The system stops escalating.

2. Reorientation

Attention slowly returns to the present.

3. Reengagement

Emotion and motivation begin to resurface.

Skipping stages delays recovery.

Why "Pushing Through" Slows Healing

Forcing productivity or emotional expression reactivates stress signals.

The system interprets pressure as danger.

Regulation requires **permission**, not demand.

Core Code for Post-Overload Stabilization

Primary Code:
541 128

This sequence supports nervous system settling after emotional saturation.

It reduces internal noise without suppressing awareness.

Application Method

- Sit or lie down comfortably
- Eyes open or closed
- Hold **541 128** mentally
- Breathe naturally
- Duration: **7–10 minutes**

No visualization required.

Signs the Code Is Working

Subtle changes may include:

- Slower breathing
- Reduced muscle tension
- A sense of "space" internally
- Less urgency in thoughts

These may appear gradually.

When to Use This Code

Most effective:

- After emotionally heavy days
- Following conflict
- During burnout recovery
- When thoughts feel crowded

Avoid using during acute panic.

Supporting Regulation Between Sessions

Helpful practices:

- Short walks
- Reduced screen exposure
- Predictable daily routines
- Hydration

Stability grows from repetition.

Important Reminder

Recovery is not linear.

Some days will feel better.
Others will not.

Both are part of regulation.

Closing Thought

Emotional overload does not require fixing.

It requires space.

In the next chapter, we will explore **rebuilding emotional resilience without stress conditioning**.

Chapter 17

Rebuilding Emotional Resilience Without Stress Conditioning**

Resilience is often misunderstood.

It is not toughness.
It is not endurance.
It is not pushing through discomfort.

True resilience is **the ability to return to baseline**.

The Problem With Stress-Based Resilience

Many people build resilience by exposing themselves to stress repeatedly.

This can work short-term.
Long-term, it conditions the nervous system to expect threat.

The system adapts by staying alert.

This is not resilience.
It is **chronic activation**.

What Healthy Resilience Actually Looks Like

Healthy resilience has three characteristics:

- Faster recovery after stress
- Lower baseline tension

- Greater emotional flexibility

It feels calm, not hardened.

Why the Nervous System Learns From Resolution, Not Stress

The nervous system learns safety **after** an experience ends.

If stress never fully resolves, the lesson is incomplete.

Repeated stress without resolution teaches:
"Danger is constant."

Resolution teaches:
"I can return."

Emotional Elasticity vs Emotional Armor

Armor blocks feeling.
Elasticity allows feeling to stretch and return.

Armor cracks.
Elasticity adapts.

Your goal is elasticity.

Core Code for Resilience Rebuilding

Primary Code:
318 517

This sequence supports emotional rebound without stimulating threat responses.

It reinforces recovery pathways instead of alert circuits.

How to Use the Code

- Sit upright or lie down
- Hold **318 517** gently in awareness
- Do not force concentration
- Duration: **8–12 minutes**

If thoughts wander, allow it.

What You May Notice

Common responses include:

- Mild emotional warmth
- Subtle confidence increase
- Less reactivity to memory triggers
- Improved tolerance for uncertainty

Effects may continue after the session.

Frequency Guidelines

Recommended:

- Once daily during recovery
- Every other day for maintenance

Do not exceed twice daily.

Supporting Emotional Elasticity

Helpful habits include:

- Ending the day calmly
- Avoiding emotional processing late at night
- Creating predictable transitions (morning and evening)

Consistency teaches safety.

What to Avoid While Rebuilding

Temporarily limit:

- Intense emotional journaling
- Over-analysis of past events
- High-stimulation media

Resilience grows quietly.

A Common Mistake

Trying to "test" resilience too soon.

If you provoke stress to see if you're better, you interrupt recovery.

Let strength show itself naturally.

Closing Thought

Resilience is not built under pressure.

It is built in the **absence of threat**.

In the next chapter, we will explore **restoring emotional motivation after numbness**.

Chapter 18

Restoring Motivation After Emotional Numbness**

Emotional numbness is not laziness.

It is not a lack of willpower.
It is not failure.

It is the nervous system conserving energy after overload.

Why Motivation Disappears After Stress

Motivation is an **output**, not a switch.

When emotional stress lasts too long, the system reduces:

- Emotional intensity
- Desire
- Drive

This prevents further depletion.

The system isn't broken.
It is protecting itself.

Why Forcing Motivation Backfires

Trying to "push through" numbness often creates:

- Irritation
- Self-judgment

- Mental fatigue

The system reads pressure as threat.

Threat deepens shutdown.

The Difference Between Drive and Readiness

Drive is energy.
Readiness is permission.

Motivation returns when the system feels safe enough to move.

Safety comes first.
Action follows.

Signs of Emotional Readiness Returning

Subtle signs include:

- Mild curiosity
- Brief interest spikes
- Desire without urgency
- Small preference formation

These moments matter.

Do not dismiss them.

Core Code for Motivation Reboot

Primary Code:
714 273

This sequence supports **emotional re-engagement** without stimulating pressure circuits.

It does not push.
It invites.

How to Use the Code

- Sit or stand comfortably
- Bring **714 273** into awareness
- Let it remain passive
- Duration: **7–10 minutes**

Do not evaluate results during the session.

What You May Experience

Common responses:

- A gentle "want" feeling
- Increased tolerance for tasks
- Reduced resistance
- Spontaneous ideas

Motivation often returns sideways.

Frequency Guidelines

- Once daily for 5–7 days
- Then reassess naturally

Stop if you feel overstimulated.

Supporting Motivation Without Pressure

Helpful actions:

- Completing very small tasks
- Ending tasks early on purpose
- Allowing incomplete progress

Momentum grows when it is allowed to stop.

What to Avoid

Avoid:

- Productivity challenges
- Timers
- "All or nothing" goals

These reactivate shutdown patterns.

A Reassuring Truth

Motivation does not need to be rebuilt.

It **returns automatically** when the system is ready.

Your role is to remove resistance, not create force.

Closing Thought

Numbness is not emptiness.

It is **paused motion**.

In the next chapter, we will address **emotional clarity after confusion and overload**.

Chapter 19

Restoring Emotional Clarity After Overload**

Emotional overload does not erase clarity.

It buries it.

Clarity returns when the system has enough space to organize again.

Why Overload Creates Confusion

When too much information enters at once, the nervous system stops sorting.

It shifts into containment mode.

Thoughts overlap.
Emotions blur.
Decisions feel impossible.

This is not indecision.
It is **protective suspension**.

Why "Thinking Harder" Makes It Worse

Trying to force clarity increases:

- Mental noise
- Frustration
- Self-doubt

The system responds by tightening further.

Clarity cannot be forced through effort.

The Role of Emotional Sorting

Clarity is a **sorting process**.

The nervous system needs:

- Quiet
- Repetition
- Predictable input

Only then can it separate signal from noise.

Signs Clarity Is Returning

Early signs include:

- Stronger preferences
- Shorter decision time
- Reduced emotional ambiguity
- Less internal debate

These signals come before certainty.

Core Code for Emotional Clarity

Primary Code:
888 412

This sequence supports emotional differentiation and cognitive quieting.

It reduces overlap rather than adding input.

How to Use the Code

- Sit quietly or walk slowly
- Hold **888 412** lightly in awareness
- Do not analyze thoughts
- Duration: **8–10 minutes**

Let clarity emerge indirectly.

What You May Notice

Common effects:

- Fewer competing thoughts
- Easier prioritization
- Less emotional static
- Subtle decisiveness

Changes are often gradual.

Frequency Guidelines

- Once daily for 4–6 days
- Pause once clarity stabilizes

Overuse can dull sensitivity.

Supporting Clarity Between Sessions

Helpful practices:

- Writing lists without solving
- Reducing choices temporarily
- Completing one thing at a time

Structure creates space.

What to Avoid During Recovery

Avoid:

- Multitasking
- Decision-heavy conversations
- Consuming excessive information

Clarity needs quiet input.

A Common Misinterpretation

People often think confusion means something is wrong.

In reality, confusion means **reorganization is underway**.

Closing Thought

Clarity is not sharpness.

It is **calm alignment**.

In the next chapter, we will focus on **emotional stability after sudden change**.

Chapter 20

Stabilizing Emotions After Sudden Change**

Sudden change destabilizes even healthy systems.

It doesn't matter whether the change is positive or negative.
The nervous system responds to **speed**, not meaning.

Why Sudden Change Feels Disorienting

When change happens too quickly, the system cannot update
expectations in real time.

This creates:

- Emotional swings
- Fatigue
- Irritability
- A sense of being "off"

This is not emotional weakness.
It is delayed integration.

The Nervous System Needs Time to Re-Map

Every major change requires internal recalibration.

The system must update:

- Safety assumptions

- Predictive models
- Emotional timing

Until this happens, instability is normal.

Why Suppressing Reactions Slows Stabilization

Ignoring emotional fluctuations teaches the system:
"This response is unsafe."

The system then holds tension longer.

Stability comes from **allowing oscillation**, not stopping it.

What Stabilization Actually Looks Like

Healthy stabilization shows up as:

- Shorter emotional spikes
- Faster return to baseline
- Less dramatic reactions
- Increased predictability

Stability is gradual, not immediate.

Core Code for Emotional Stabilization

Primary Code:
404 931

This sequence supports emotional settling after rapid change.

It helps the system recalibrate without forcing calm.

How to Use the Code

- Sit comfortably with feet grounded
- Hold **404 931** gently in awareness
- No visualization required
- Duration: **8–12 minutes**

Allow sensations to rise and fall.

What You May Experience

Common responses include:

- A sense of "landing"
- Reduced emotional whiplash
- Improved sleep onset
- Less reactive thinking

Some people notice effects the following day.

Frequency Guidelines

- Once daily during periods of change
- Reduce to every other day as stability returns

Discontinue if emotional flattening occurs.

Supporting Stabilization in Daily Life

Helpful behaviors:

- Keeping routines simple
- Avoiding big decisions temporarily
- Maintaining consistent sleep and meals

Predictability restores balance.

What to Avoid

Avoid:

- Rapid new commitments
- Major emotional processing
- Drastic lifestyle changes

Stability needs space.

A Critical Reminder

You do not need to "adjust faster."

Your system will stabilize **at its own pace**.

Rushing only extends instability.

Closing Thought

Stability is not rigidity.

It is **flexibility with a reliable center**.

This concludes the core chapter sequence.

Next, we move into **Appendices and integration guidance**.

Appendix A

Relapse Warning Signals**

Relapse does not begin with behavior.
It begins with **subtle internal shifts**.

Learning to recognize early signals prevents regression before it takes hold.

What "Relapse" Actually Means

Relapse is not failure.

It is a **temporary loss of regulation** caused by overload, neglect, or misalignment.

Most relapses are preventable when caught early.

Early Emotional Warning Signals

Common early signs include:

- Increased irritability without clear cause
- Emotional numbness or flattening
- Heightened sensitivity to small stressors
- Sudden fatigue after social interaction

These signals indicate nervous system strain.

Cognitive Warning Signals

Watch for:

- Repetitive negative thinking
- Loss of mental clarity
- Difficulty making simple decisions
- Increased self-criticism

This is cognitive overload, not loss of progress.

Physical Warning Signals

The body often reacts first.

Early physical signs:

- Sleep disruption
- Tight jaw or shoulders
- Shallow breathing
- Digestive changes

Physical signals should never be ignored.

Behavioral Warning Signals

Behavior shifts often appear last:

- Avoidance of routines
- Withdrawal from supportive habits
- Overworking or under-functioning
- Seeking distraction instead of rest

These indicate depletion, not laziness.

The Most Overlooked Signal

The most common warning sign is:

"I don't need to do the basics anymore."

This belief usually appears **before** a downturn.

Immediate Response Protocol

If two or more warning signals appear:

1. Pause new commitments
2. Reduce stimulation
3. Restore sleep and nutrition
4. Resume grounding practices

Do not push forward.

Stabilize first.

Stabilization Support Code

Primary Support Code:
918 744

This sequence supports rapid nervous system re-balancing during early relapse signs.

Use once daily for **5–7 days**.

When to Resume Normal Practice

Return to regular practice only when:

- Emotional baseline is steady
- Sleep has normalized
- Cognitive clarity returns

Progress resumes from stability.

What Relapse Is *Not*

Relapse is not:

- A reset to zero
- Proof something "stopped working"
- A personal failure

It is feedback.

Final Reminder

Your system is adaptive.

Early awareness prevents long recovery cycles.

Listening early is strength.

Appendix B

Daily Stabilization & Reset Protocol**

This protocol is designed for **maintenance, recovery, and recalibration**.

Use it when life becomes noisy, progress feels unstable, or consistency slips.

Purpose of the Reset Protocol

The goal is not acceleration.

The goal is **stability first**, momentum second.

This protocol restores baseline balance so advanced practices remain effective.

When to Use This Protocol

Use this protocol when:

- Emotional reactivity increases
- Sleep quality declines
- Focus becomes inconsistent
- Motivation fluctuates

It is preventative, not corrective.

The 5-Step Daily Reset

Complete once per day, preferably in the morning or early evening.

Step 1 — Ground the Body

Sit comfortably.
Feet flat on the floor.
Slow breathing for 2–3 minutes.

No visualization required.

Step 2 — Stabilization Sequence

Read or repeat silently:

714
328
990

Pause briefly between each sequence.

This supports nervous system coherence and mental steadiness.

Step 3 — Emotional Neutralization

Place attention on the chest area.

Repeat the following internally for one minute:

"I am safe in this moment."

Do not force emotion.
Allow neutrality.

Step 4 — Cognitive Clearing

Identify one lingering thought.

Do not analyze it.

Simply acknowledge it and release it.

This step prevents mental accumulation.

Step 5 — Intent Re-Alignment

End with a single, simple intention for the day.

Examples:

- "Steady."
- "Calm."
- "Clarity."

Keep it brief.

Duration Guidelines

- Minimum: **3 consecutive days**
- Recommended: **7 days**
- Maximum: **14 days**

Longer use is unnecessary unless under sustained stress.

Common Mistakes to Avoid

- Skipping days
- Adding extra techniques
- Treating the protocol as a task instead of support

Simplicity is what makes it effective.

Supportive Stabilization Code

Supplementary Code:
440 121

Use only if anxiety or restlessness persists after Step 2.

Signs the Reset Is Working

You may notice:

- Improved sleep
- Reduced emotional spikes
- Clearer thinking
- Increased patience

These indicate baseline recovery.

Transitioning Back to Full Practice

When stability returns:

- Resume normal chapter practices gradually
- Do not "catch up" aggressively
- Maintain one daily grounding habit

Stability compounds progress.

Final Note

Consistency matters more than intensity.

Resetting is not retreating.

It is intelligent self-regulation.

Final Notes from the Author

This book was never meant to promise miracles.

It was meant to offer **structure**, **consistency**, and **personal responsibility** in a world that often looks for shortcuts.

The practices in these pages are simple by design.
Simplicity is not weakness — it is what makes repetition possible, and repetition is where change actually happens.

A Grounded Reminder

Nothing here replaces:

- medical care
- professional advice
- personal accountability

This work is **complementary**, not corrective.

Use it to support your wellbeing, not to avoid real-world action.

About Consistency

Progress rarely arrives as a sudden shift.

More often, it shows up quietly:

- fewer bad days
- shorter setbacks
- faster emotional recovery

- clearer thinking

These are wins.
Do not overlook them.

If You Stop Practicing

That's fine.

Life happens.

When you return:

- start small
- use fewer sequences
- rebuild rhythm before intensity

There is no penalty for pausing.

If You Continue

Approach this work with:

- calm curiosity
- patience
- respect for your own limits

There is no finish line here — only refinement.

A Final Thought

Your body already knows how to heal.
Your mind already knows how to settle.

This book simply gives you a **language for consistency**.

Nothing more.
Nothing less.

Thank you for trusting yourself enough to begin.

— **James Hutchinson**